Math Fun with Puppies and Kittens

Learning SUBTRACTION with Puppies and Kittens

Eustacia Moldovo
and Patricia J. Murphy

Enslow Publishing
101 W. 23rd Street
Suite 240
New York, NY 10011
USA
enslow.com

Words to Know

basic Simplest.

difference The answer to a subtraction fact.

equal Of the same value.

minuend The first number in a subtraction fact.

operation A way to get one number using other numbers by following special rules.

subtrahend The second number in a subtraction fact.

value The amount or worth of something.

Contents

Words to Know 2
Subtraction 4
Learn to Subtract 0 6
Learn to Subtract 1 8
Learn to Subtract 2 10
Learn to Subtract 3 12
Learn to Subtract 4 14
Learn to Subtract 5 16
Learn to Subtract 6 18
Learn to Subtract 7 20
Learn to Subtract 8 22
Learn to Subtract 9 24
Learn to Subtract 10 26
Review Subtraction Facts 28
Activities with Subtraction 30
Learn More 31
Index 32

Subtraction

Subtraction is the kind of math you use to take one number away from another. The answer is called the **difference**. The difference tells you how many things you have left. You can count puppies and kittens to learn how subtraction works!

11 – 5 = 6 is called a subtraction fact.

$$11 - 5 = 6$$

There are two ways to write subtraction facts:

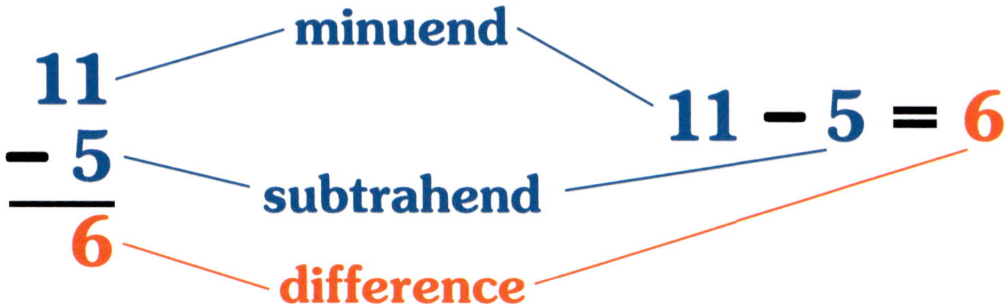

There are five parts to a subtraction fact:

(1) The **minuend** is the number you start with: **11**.

(2) The minus sign (–) means subtract.

(3) The **subtrahend** is the number you take away from the minuend: **5**.

(4) An **equal** sign (= or ___).

(5) The difference after the equal sign: **6**.

You read this subtraction fact as "Eleven minus five equals six," or "Eleven take away five equals six."

Four Math Operations

Subtraction is one of the four basic operations used in math. The other three are addition, multiplication, and division.

Learn to Subtract 0

Let's start with the number **0**. If you subtract **0** from any number, the answer will always equal that number. Nothing changes because **0** has no **value**.

5 – 0

Five (**5**) kittens swat the toy. Zero (**0**) kittens stop playing. How many kittens play?

Number Lines

Number lines make subtracting easier. Start at the minuend. Then move back the number of spaces equal to the subtrahend. You will land on the difference.

0 – 0 = 0
1 – 0 = 1
2 – 0 = 2
3 – 0 = 3
4 – 0 = 4
5 – 0 = 5
6 – 0 = 6
7 – 0 = 7
8 – 0 = 8
9 – 0 = 9
10 – 0 = 10
11 – 0 = 11
12 – 0 = 12
13 – 0 = 13
14 – 0 = 14
15 – 0 = 15
16 – 0 = 16
17 – 0 = 17
18 – 0 = 18
19 – 0 = 19
20 – 0 = 20

=

5

Begin at **5**. Move **0** spaces to the left. The difference is **5** because you did not go anywhere on the number line.

Learn to Subtract 1

When you subtract **1** from any number, the answer will always be one less than that number.

7 – 1

Seven (7) puppies take a nap. One (1) puppy wakes up.

How many puppies are still asleep?

= **6**

Begin at **7**. Move **1** space to the left.
The difference is **6**.

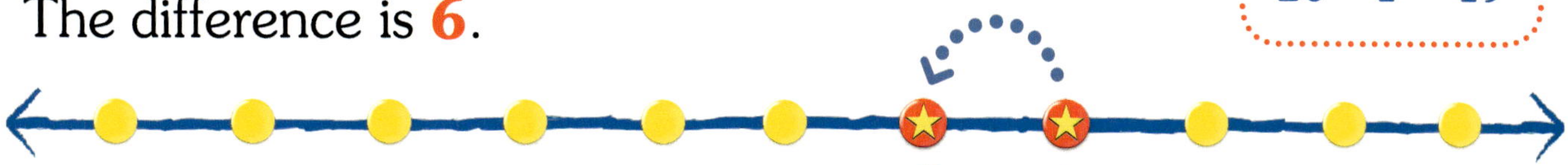

1 − 1 = 0
2 − 1 = 1
3 − 1 = 2
4 − 1 = 3
5 − 1 = 4
6 − 1 = 5
7 − 1 = 6
8 − 1 = 7
9 − 1 = 8
10 − 1 = 9
11 − 1 = 10
12 − 1 = 11
13 − 1 = 12
14 − 1 = 13
15 − 1 = 14
16 − 1 = 15
17 − 1 = 16
18 − 1 = 17
19 − 1 = 18
20 − 1 = 19

Learn to Subtract 2

Counting back is one way to find the difference when you are subtracting more than 1. Count back with things or a number line. To solve **5 – 2**, count back with kittens. Begin with **5**. Then count back two (**2**) numbers.

5 – 2

Five (**5**) kittens are on the bed. Two (**2**) kittens jump off.

How many kittens are left on the bed?

=

3

2 – 2 =	0
3 – 2 =	1
4 – 2 =	2
5 – 2 =	**3**
6 – 2 =	4
7 – 2 =	5
8 – 2 =	6
9 – 2 =	7
10 – 2 =	8
11 – 2 =	9
12 – 2 =	10
13 – 2 =	11
14 – 2 =	12
15 – 2 =	13
16 – 2 =	14
17 – 2 =	15
18 – 2 =	16
19 – 2 =	17
20 – 2 =	18

Begin at **5**. Move **2** spaces to the left.
The difference is **3**.

Learn to Subtract 3

The subtraction fact **6 − 3** is called a doubles fact. The subtrahend is half the minuend. The difference is the same as the subtrahend.

Six (**6**) puppies sit on the floor. Three (**3**) puppies get up and walk away. How many puppies are still sitting?

Ten Doubles Facts

You will know ten new subtraction facts when you learn these doubles:

2 – 1 = 1
4 – 2 = 2
6 – 3 = 3
8 – 4 = 4
10 – 5 = 5

12 – 6 = 6
14 – 7 = 7
16 – 8 = 8
18 – 9 = 9
20 – 10 = 10

3 – 3 = 0
4 – 3 = 1
5 – 3 = 2
6 – 3 = 3
7 – 3 = 4
8 – 3 = 5
9 – 3 = 6
10 – 3 = 7
11 – 3 = 8
12 – 3 = 9
13 – 3 = 10
14 – 3 = 11
15 – 3 = 12
16 – 3 = 13
17 – 3 = 14
18 – 3 = 15
19 – 3 = 16
20 – 3 = 17

=

3

Begin at **6**. Move **3** spaces to the left.
The difference is **3**.

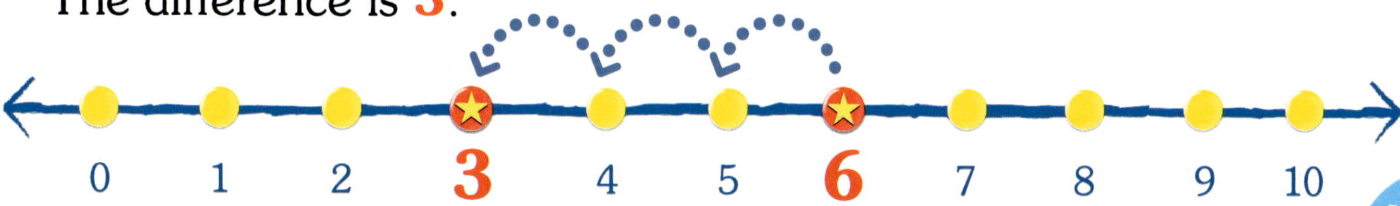

Learn to Subtract 4

When you subtract two even numbers, the difference will be even. The number **10** is even. The number **4** is also even.

10 – 4

Ten (**10**) kittens go to the veterinarian. Four (**4**) kittens get their checkups. How many kittens still need their checkups?

Even Numbers

An even number of kittens comes in pairs. But 0 is an even number, too. Even numbers are 0, 2, 4, 6, 8, 10, 12, 14, 16, 18, 20, and so on.

4 – 4 = 0
5 – 4 = 1
6 – 4 = 2
7 – 4 = 3
8 – 4 = 4
9 – 4 = 5
10 – 4 = 6
11 – 4 = 7
12 – 4 = 8
13 – 4 = 9
14 – 4 = 10
15 – 4 = 11
16 – 4 = 12
17 – 4 = 13
18 – 4 = 14
19 – 4 = 15
20 – 4 = 16

=

6

Begin at **10**. Move **4** spaces to the left. The difference is **6**, which is even, too.

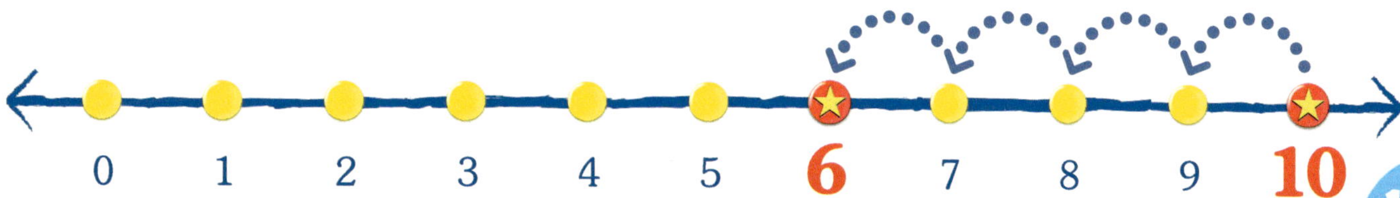

Learn to Subtract 5

When you subtract two odd numbers, the difference will always be even. The number **9** is odd. The number **5** is also odd.

9 – 5

Nine (**9**) puppies go to the groomer. Five (**5**) puppies get their fur trimmed. How many puppies are still waiting for their haircuts?

=

4

Begin at **9**. Move **5** spaces to the left. The difference is **4**, which is even.

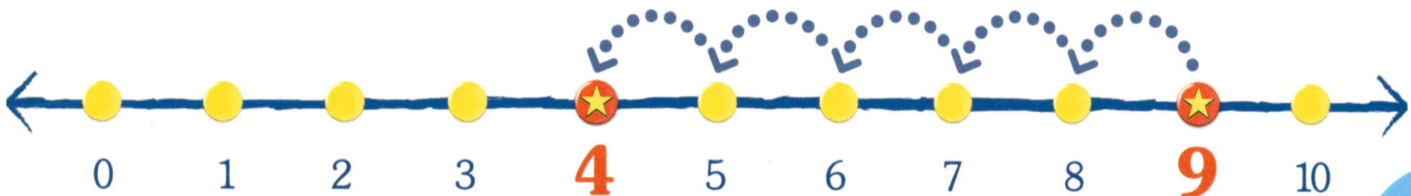

5 – 5 = 0
6 – 5 = 1
7 – 5 = 2
8 – 5 = 3
9 – 5 = 4
10 – 5 = 5
11 – 5 = 6
12 – 5 = 7
13 – 5 = 8
14 – 5 = 9
15 – 5 = 10
16 – 5 = 11
17 – 5 = 12
18 – 5 = 13
19 – 5 = 14
20 – 5 = 15

Learn to Subtract 6

When a subtraction fact has an even number and an odd number, the difference will always be odd. The number **11** is odd. The number **6** is even.

11 – 6

11 – 6

Eleven (**11**) kittens eat cat food. Six (**6**) kittens finish their meals. How many kittens are still eating?

$6 - 6 = 0$
$7 - 6 = 1$
$8 - 6 = 2$
$9 - 6 = 3$
$10 - 6 = 4$
$\mathbf{11 - 6 = 5}$
$12 - 6 = 6$
$13 - 6 = 7$
$14 - 6 = 8$
$15 - 6 = 9$
$16 - 6 = 10$
$17 - 6 = 11$
$18 - 6 = 12$
$19 - 6 = 13$
$20 - 6 = 14$

=

5

Begin at **11**. Move **6** spaces to the left. The difference is **5**.

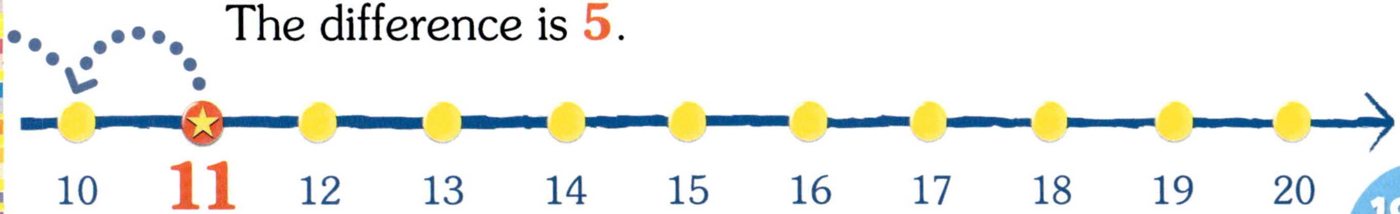

Learn to Subtract 7

You can use addition facts to solve subtraction facts. Try it with **15 – 7**. If you remember **7 + 8 = 15**, then you can figure out **15 – 7 = 8**.

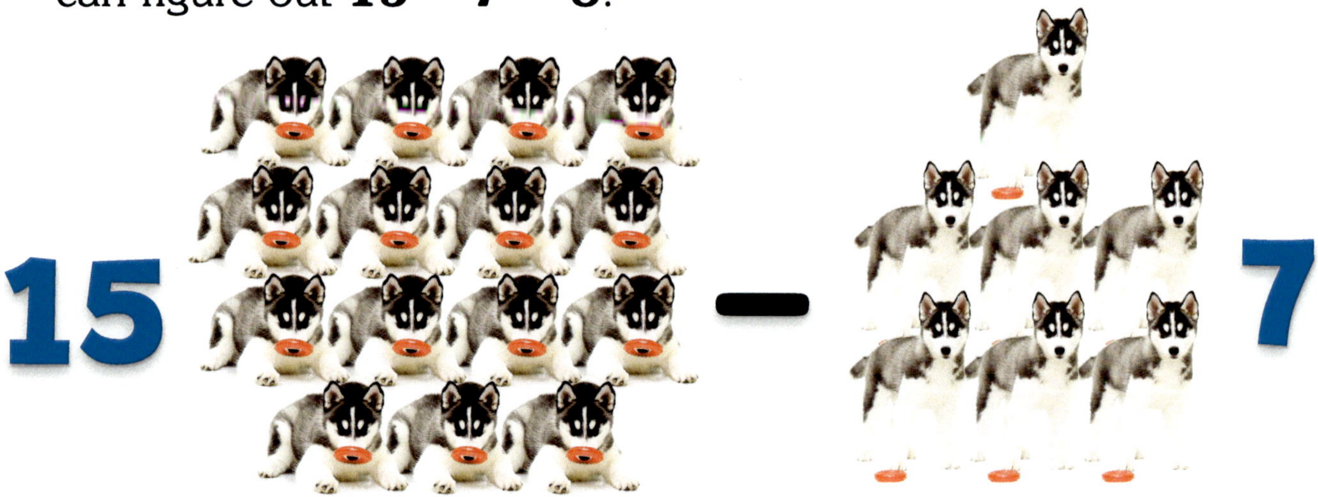

Fifteen (**15**) puppies play with their toys. Seven (**7**) puppies get bored and leave. How many puppies keep playing?

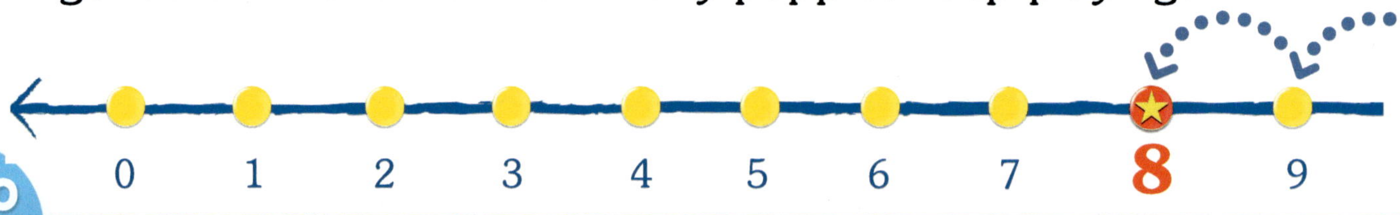

Fact Families

Subtraction facts and addition facts that are related are called fact families. When you learn one of these math facts, you really learn four facts! For example:

15 – 7 = 8
15 – 8 = 7
7 + 8 = 15
8 + 7 = 15

7 – 7 = 0
8 – 7 = 1
9 – 7 = 2
10 – 7 = 3
11 – 7 = 4
12 – 7 = 5
13 – 7 = 6
14 – 7 = 7
15 – 7 = 8
16 – 7 = 9
17 – 7 = 10
18 – 7 = 11
19 – 7 = 12
20 – 7 = 13

=

8

Begin at **15**. Move **7** spaces to the left. The difference is **8**.

Learn to Subtract 8

You already learned to count back to solve subtraction facts. You can also count on to find answers to subtraction problems. Try it with **10 – 8**.

–

10 **8**

Ten (**10**) kittens cuddle together. Eight (**8**) kittens get up to explore the room. How many kittens are left cuddling together?

Start with the smaller number, **8**. Then count up to **10**. The difference is **2** because you had to count up two numbers to move from 8 to 10.

= **2**

8 – 8 = 0
9 – 8 = 1
10 – 8 = 2
11 – 8 = 3
12 – 8 = 4
13 – 8 = 5
14 – 8 = 6
15 – 8 = 7
16 – 8 = 8
17 – 8 = 9
18 – 8 = 10
19 – 8 = 11
20 – 8 = 12

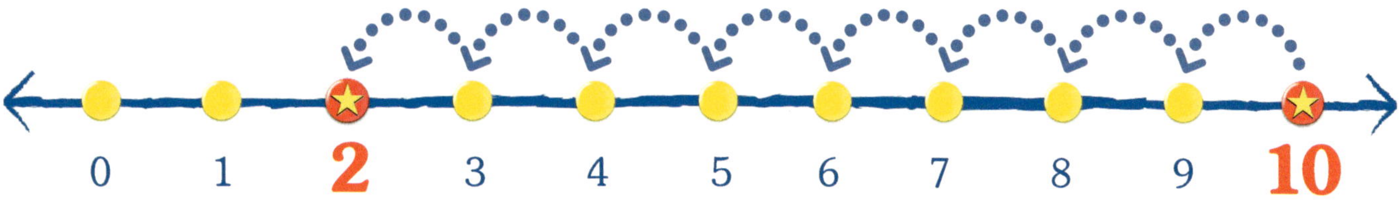

Double check your answer using the number line. Begin at **10**. Move **8** spaces to the left. The difference is **2**.

Learn to Subtract 9

Now that you have learned all the different ways to do subtraction, can you solve **16 – 9**?

Sixteen (**16**) puppies bark. Nine (**9**) puppies stop barking. How many puppies keep barking?

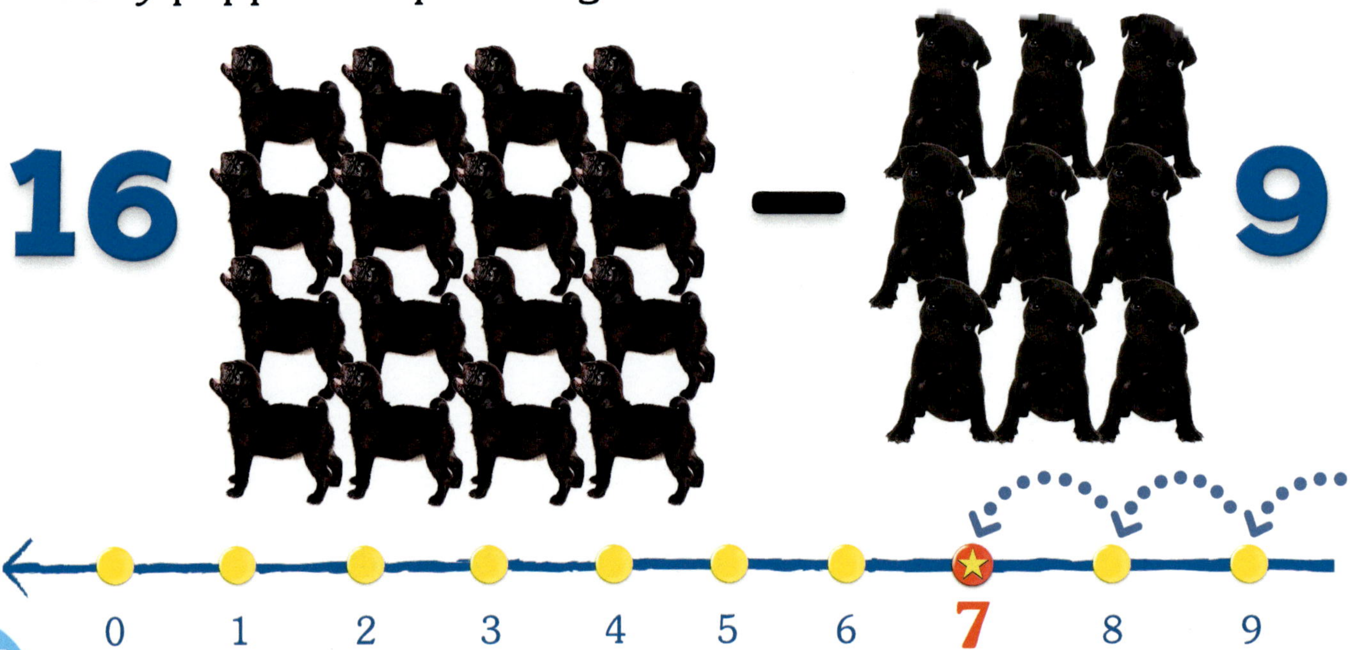

Ten Is the Magic Number

Another way to solve subtraction problems is to break down numbers leading to a 10. For example:

$16 - 9 = 16 - 6 - 3 = 10 - 3 = 7$

$9 - 9 = 0$
$10 - 9 = 1$
$11 - 9 = 2$
$12 - 9 = 3$
$13 - 9 = 4$
$14 - 9 = 5$
$15 - 9 = 6$
$16 - 9 = 7$
$17 - 9 = 8$
$18 - 9 = 9$
$19 - 9 = 10$
$20 - 9 = 11$

=

7

Begin at **16**. Move **9** spaces to the left. The difference is **7**.

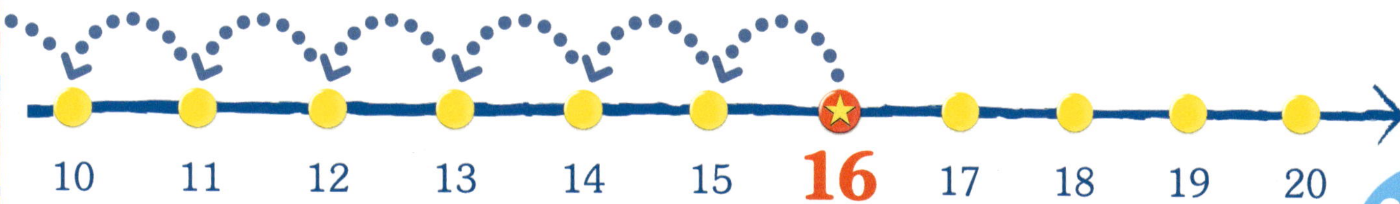

Learn to Subtract 10

Try another one! What is the difference between **20** and **10**?

20 − 10

You have twenty (**20**) kittens. Ten (**10**) kittens greet you at the door. How many kittens hide?

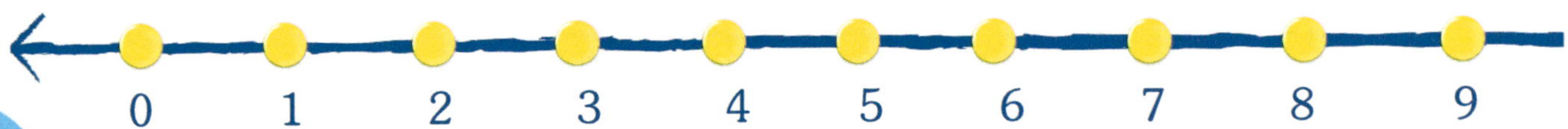

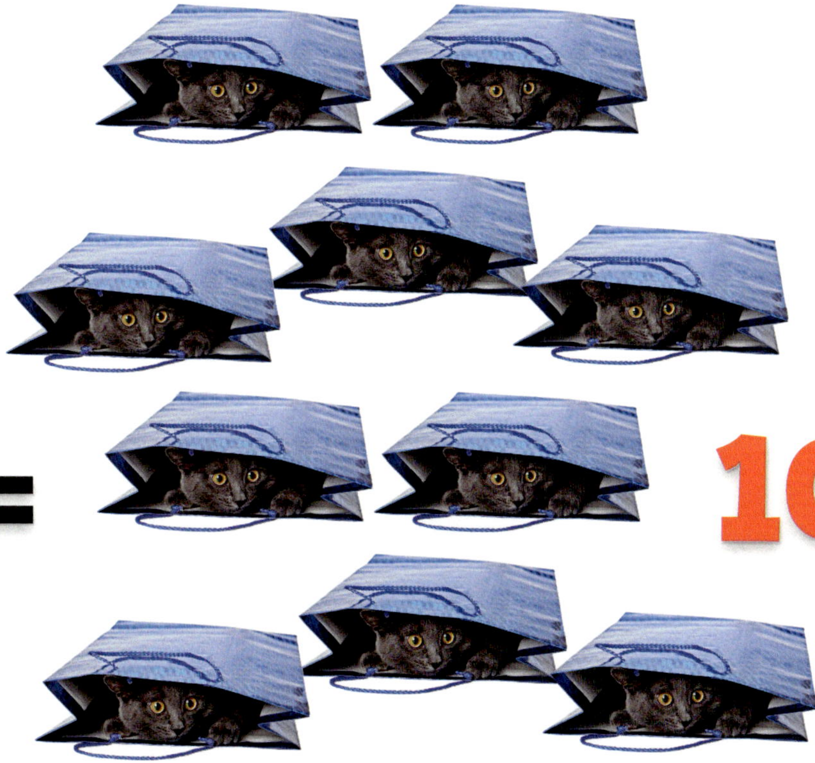

= 10

10 – 10 = 0
11 – 10 = 1
12 – 10 = 2
13 – 10 = 3
14 – 10 = 4
15 – 10 = 5
16 – 10 = 6
17 – 10 = 7
18 – 10 = 8
19 – 10 = 9
20 – 10 = 10

Begin at **20**. Move **10** spaces to the left. The difference is **10**.

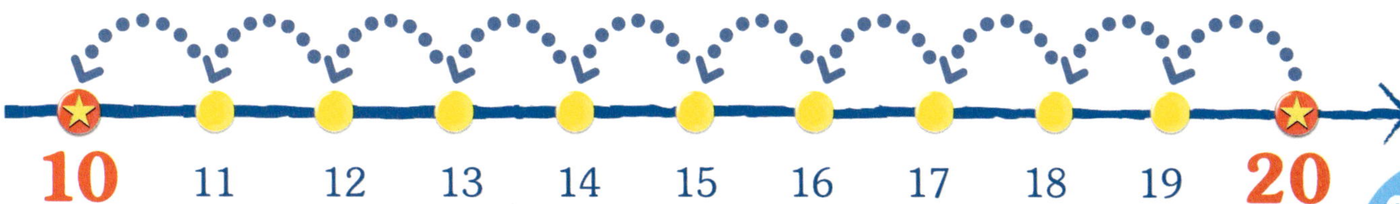

Review Subtraction Facts

Do you know all the subtraction facts in this book? Take a look!

- 0	- 1	- 2	- 3	- 4	- 5
0 - 0 = 0	1 - 1 = 0	2 - 2 = 0	3 - 3 = 0	4 - 4 = 0	5 - 5 = 0
1 - 0 = 1	2 - 1 = 1	3 - 2 = 1	4 - 3 = 1	5 - 4 = 1	6 - 5 = 1
2 - 0 = 2	3 - 1 = 2	4 - 2 = 2	5 - 3 = 2	6 - 4 = 2	7 - 5 = 2
3 - 0 = 3	4 - 1 = 3	5 - 2 = 3	6 - 3 = 3	7 - 4 = 3	8 - 5 = 3
4 - 0 = 4	5 - 1 = 4	6 - 2 = 4	7 - 3 = 4	8 - 4 = 4	9 - 5 = 4
5 - 0 = 5	6 - 1 = 5	7 - 2 = 5	8 - 3 = 5	9 - 4 = 5	10 - 5 = 5
6 - 0 = 6	7 - 1 = 6	8 - 2 = 6	9 - 3 = 6	10 - 4 = 6	11 - 5 = 6
7 - 0 = 7	8 - 1 = 7	9 - 2 = 7	10 - 3 = 7	11 - 4 = 7	12 - 5 = 7
8 - 0 = 8	9 - 1 = 8	10 - 2 = 8	11 - 3 = 8	12 - 4 = 8	13 - 5 = 8
9 - 0 = 9	10 - 1 = 9	11 - 2 = 9	12 - 3 = 9	13 - 4 = 9	14 - 5 = 9
10 - 0 = 10	11 - 1 = 10	12 - 2 = 10	13 - 3 = 10	14 - 4 = 10	15 - 5 = 10
11 - 0 = 11	12 - 1 = 11	13 - 2 = 11	14 - 3 = 11	15 - 4 = 11	16 - 5 = 11
12 - 0 = 12	13 - 1 = 12	14 - 2 = 12	15 - 3 = 12	16 - 4 = 12	17 - 5 = 12
13 - 0 = 13	14 - 1 = 13	15 - 2 = 13	16 - 3 = 13	17 - 4 = 13	18 - 5 = 13
14 - 0 = 14	15 - 1 = 14	16 - 2 = 14	17 - 3 = 14	18 - 4 = 14	19 - 5 = 14
15 - 0 = 15	16 - 1 = 15	17 - 2 = 15	18 - 3 = 15	19 - 4 = 15	20 - 5 = 15
16 - 0 = 16	17 - 1 = 16	18 - 2 = 16	19 - 3 = 16	20 - 4 = 16	
17 - 0 = 17	18 - 1 = 17	19 - 2 = 17	20 - 3 = 17		
18 - 0 = 18	19 - 1 = 18	20 - 2 = 18			
19 - 0 = 19	20 - 1 = 19				
20 - 0 = 20					

- 6	- 7	- 8	- 9	- 10	Doubles
6 - 6 = 0	7 - 7 = 0	8 - 8 = 0	9 - 9 = 0	10 - 10 = 0	0 - 0 = 0
7 - 6 = 1	8 - 7 = 1	9 - 8 = 1	10 - 9 = 1	11 - 10 = 1	2 - 1 = 1
8 - 6 = 2	9 - 7 = 2	10 - 8 = 2	11 - 9 = 2	12 - 10 = 2	4 - 2 = 2
9 - 6 = 3	10 - 7 = 3	11 - 8 = 3	12 - 9 = 3	13 - 10 = 3	6 - 3 = 3
10 - 6 = 4	11 - 7 = 4	12 - 8 = 4	13 - 9 = 4	14 - 10 = 4	8 - 4 = 4
11 - 6 = 5	12 - 7 = 5	13 - 8 = 5	14 - 9 = 5	15 - 10 = 5	10 - 5 = 5
12 - 6 = 6	13 - 7 = 6	14 - 8 = 6	15 - 9 = 6	16 - 10 = 6	12 - 6 = 6
13 - 6 = 7	14 - 7 = 7	15 - 8 = 7	16 - 9 = 7	17 - 10 = 7	14 - 7 = 7
14 - 6 = 8	15 - 7 = 8	16 - 8 = 8	17 - 9 = 8	18 - 10 = 8	16 - 8 = 8
15 - 6 = 9	16 - 7 = 9	17 - 8 = 9	18 - 9 = 9	19 - 10 = 9	18 - 9 = 9
16 - 6 = 10	17 - 7 = 10	18 - 8 = 10	19 - 9 = 10	20 - 10 = 10	20 - 10 = 10
17 - 6 = 11	18 - 7 = 11	19 - 8 = 11	20 - 9 = 11		
18 - 6 = 12	19 - 7 = 12	20 - 8 = 12			
19 - 6 = 13	20 - 7 = 13				
20 - 6 = 14					

Activities with Subtraction

Make Flashcards

Write a subtraction fact on one side of an index card. Write the answer on the other side. Make as many cards as you want. Now test yourself! How many did you get right?

Subtract Things Around the House

Numbers are everywhere you look. Subtract the number of hats from the number of pants you have. Subtract money, toys, or anything you want!

Create a Quiz

List five different subtraction facts without the differences on a piece of paper. Have a friend solve the problems. Check your friend's answers by looking in this book. Did your friend pass the quiz?

Write a Story

Write your own story using a subtraction fact. For example:

Nina had 16 marbles. She gave 5 of them to her friend Frankie. Nina has 11 marbles left.

You can make it as long or as short as you want. You can even draw pictures to go with your story!

Learn More

Books

First, Rachel. ***Subtract It! Fun with Subtraction.*** North Mankato, MN: Sandcastle, 2016.

Hamilton, Lily. ***Helping at the Race: Subtraction Within 20.*** New York, NY: Rosen Classroom, 2015.

Summers, Portia. ***Subtracting Coins and Bills.*** New York, NY: Enslow Publishing, 2016.

Websites

ABCYa.com

www.abcya.com/first_grade_computers.htm#numbers-cat

Play games to practice math!

Doctor Genius, Subtraction

www.mathabc.com/math-1st-grade/subtraction/subtraction-up-to-20

Solve subtraction problems online!

Math Playground

www.mathplayground.com/grade_1_games.html

Here are more fun math games!

Index

doubles fact, 12, 13
equal sign, 5
even numbers, 14, 15, 16, 17, 18,
fact families, 21
minuend, 5, 7, 12
minus sign, 5
number lines, 7, 10, 23
odd numbers, 16, 18
operations, 5
subtraction fact, 4, 5, 12, 13, 18, 19, 21, 22, 28–29
subtrahend, 5, 7, 12

Published in 2018 by Enslow Publishing, LLC.
101 W. 23rd Street, Suite 240, New York, NY 10011

Library of Congress Cataloging-in-Publication Data

Names: Moldovo, Eustacia, author. | Murphy, Patricia J., 1963- author.
Title: Learning subtraction with puppies and kittens / Eustacia Moldovo and Patricia J. Murphy.
Description: New York, NY : Enslow Publishing, 2018. | Series: Math fun with puppies and kittens | Audience: K to grade 3. | Includes bibliographical references and index.
Identifiers: LCCN 2017013526 | ISBN 9780766090903 (library bound) | ISBN 9780766090712 (pbk.) | ISBN 9780766090767 (6 pack)
Subjects: LCSH: Subtraction—Juvenile literature. | Mathematics—Juvenile literature.
Classification: LCC QA115 .M648 2018 | DDC 513.2/12—dc23
LC record available at https://lccn.loc.gov/2017013526

Printed in China

Portions of this book appeared in the book *Subtracting Puppies and Kittens*.

Photo credits: Cover, p. 1 (kitten, left) Bartkowski/Shutterstock.com; cover, p. 1 (kitten, center) Andrey_Kuzmin/Shutterstock.com; cover, p. 1 (puppy) WilleeCole Photography/Shutterstock.com; pp. 2 (kitten, far left), 25 (kitten) Happy monkey/Shutterstock.com; p. 2 (puppy, left) Liliya Kulianionak/Shutterstock.com; p. 2 (other animals) Ermolaev Alexander/Shutterstock.com; p. 4 (puppies) Vivienstock/Shutterstock.com; p. 4 (kittens) Eric Isselee/Shutterstock.com; p. 5 Tatiana Katsai/Shutterstock.com; pp. 6, 7 (kitten with toy) Tony Campbell/Shutterstock.com; p. 7 (kitten, top) Lubava/Shutterstock.com; pp. 8, 9 (puppies) Viorel Sima/Shutterstock.com; pp. 10, 11 (kittens) WilleeCole Photography/Shutterstock.com; pp. 10, 11 (bed) Dima Moroz/Shutterstock.com; pp. 12, 13 (beagle puppies) Fesus Robert/Shutterstock.com; p. 13 (puppy, top) ARTSILENSE/Shutterstock.com; pp. 14, 15 (sitting kittens) Andrey_Kuzmin/Shutterstock.com; p. 14 (kitten and woman) Ermolaev Alexander/Shutterstock.com; p. 15 yevgeniy11/Shutterstock.com; pp. 16, 17 (puppies) Konstantin Gushcha/Shutterstock.com; pp. 18, 19 (kittens with dishes) S-F/Shutterstock.com; pp. 20, 21 (Siberian husky puppies) Sbolotova/Shutterstock.com; pp. 22, 23 (cuddling kittens) Tony Campbell/Shutterstock.com; p. 22 (black kitten, walking) Eric Isselee/Shutterstock.com; p. 22 (yellow kitten, walking) Irina oxilixo Danilova/Shutterstock.com; pp. 24, 25 (black pug, barking) Mila Atkovska/Shutterstock.com; p. 24 (black pug, staring) cynoclub/Shutterstock.com; pp. 26 (kittens in bed), 27 (kitten in bag) linavita/Shutterstock.com; p. 26 (kittens, sitting) Utekhina Anna/Shutterstock.com; p. 29 (animals) Liliya Kulianionak/Shutterstock.com.